A GLIMPSE OF THE BIG LGHT: LOSING PARENTS, FINDING SPIRIT.

Copyright © 2005 by Harvey Wasserman. All rights reserved.
Printed in the United States of America. No part of this book may be used or reproduced in any manner whatsoever without written permission except in the case of brief quotations embodied in critical articles and reviews. For information address: www.harveywasserman.com. Box 23032; Columbus, Ohio 43223; windhw@aol.com.

If you have received this in 2004, it is an author's proof.
First edition published January 2005.

Designed by Charlie Einhorn (www.innerart.com) and Harvey Wasserman

Cover design by Charlie Einhorn, Adam Einhorn and Harvey Wasserman.
Back cover photo of Harvey Wasserman by Annie Wasserman.
Back cover photos: Sig and Phyllis Wasserman with Harvey, circa 1946; Harvey at Montague Farm, circa 1970; Harvey and Susan Wasserman married by Rabbi Shlomo Carlebach, 1988; Sig and Phyllis with grandchildren Annie, Abbie and Julie, circa 1993.
Additional photos are of Shoshanna Wasserman and Rachel Rosenblum (Greenblatt).
Library of Congress Cataloging-in-Publication Data is available. ISBN#0-97534402-2-0.

A GLIMPSE OF THE BIG LIGHT

Losing Parents, Finding Spirit
By Harvey Wasserman

Introduction by Marianne Williamson

"A knockout...a seductive and important piece of work...The process of creating it must have been the most terrific high imaginable"
...**Kurt Vonnegut**

"This beautiful poem is a powerful rite of passage. For all who struggle with the passing of parents and the quest for spirit, it's a song for the soul"
... **Bonnie Raitt**

"Touching and wonderful" ...**Ed Asner**

"Beautiful poetry from a noble soul" ...**Dr. Helen Caldicott**

"In this poem of light and death, Harvey Wasserman...bears eloquent and moving witness to his own personal awakening, and how that has fueled his passion to transform the world around him"   ...**Bernie Glassman, Roshi**

"An inspiring political activist and writer takes a deep and loving look at his inner life" ...**Alicia Bay Laurel**

"An eye-opening experience of the love sewn into the Universe"
... **Michael O'Keefe**

"A beautiful work"
... **Ina Mae Gaskin**

Thanks!

… to our wonderful family and friends, all of you, for unending love and support;
… to our various communities;
… to those of you kind enough to read and listen and improve this poem;
… to Charlie and Adam Einhorn for setting it up for publication;
… to all those who work, against all apparent odds, for peace, justice, environmental sanity and spiritual liberation;
… to Emily Dickinson, for reminding us to "trade all you have or might have been for one small breath of ecstasy";
… and to you, dear reader, for being who you are.

ISHALAMBUDDHILA!!

This is Dedicated to the One-Eye Love

A GLIMPSE OF THE BIG LIGHT

Losing Parents, Finding Spirit

Introduction

Harvey Wasserman has lived an almost mythic life.

His joys and sorrows, wins and losses, dot a journey that typifies a particular time and place.

His deep and passionate love for his family, his commitment to a better world, his continuing journey as a healer of the planet — he's like a human torch that doesn't burn out. It's fueled by an internal fire that is clearly lit by an otherworldly hand.

I wonder, thinking about someone like Harvey, where all that fire comes from. Now, having read *A Glimpse of the Big Light*, I think I know.

The greatest gift of Harvey's life, to those of us who are blessed by its fruits, is that he holds within himself the ultimate juxtaposition: the tragedy of the world that is, combined with the glory of the world that could be. Like the classic Tevye in *The Fiddler on the Roof*, he both praises God and rages at Him at the same time. Why is it this way, when it could be that way?

It is an extraordinary soul that stays awake to that question, that refuses to stop asking it, that refuses to surrender to the mediocrity and complacency the mere stress of asking it can produce over time.

Many of us started out with Harvey's passion. Thirty years later, however, so many among us have given up. That is why his passion inspires us now more than ever. He looks the disappointments of our age so clearly in the eye. His gift is that he doesn't shrink from what is.

In *A Glimpse of the Big Light*, we get a clue as to why.

Reading of his relationship with his parents, we understand more clearly our relationship with our own.

Reading of his relation to his roots, we understand more clearly our relation to our own. Reading of his ability to care, to strive, and to cry his own tears - we understand more deeply our need to cry our own.

I began the book assuming that the Big Light was the light of God. Having read it, I get that it's the light in Harvey.

The book makes the point unmistakably clear: the light in God is the light in the man. That's where all that fire comes from. And that's why it will not go out.

May all of us catch a glimpse of that light, and shine on and on and on and on….

———*Marianne Williamson*

Prologue

JULIANNA'S WORLD

*The lush warm waters
of the Gulf of Mexico
have regained their composure
after the wild turbulations
of a much-appreciated
summer storm.*

*We face them
or I do
my upper torso
infinitely enhanced
by the grace
of Julianna.*

*Her chunk of a body
makes my chest glow.*

*Her ruby heart
wanders into mine
resonating with
the consonance of souls.*

*Daddy and daughter
parent and child
our blood
co-mingled by gene
now rejoins
like two streams to a river.*

*What a powerful fusion
when they touch!*

What glorious lightening!

*Each night
the strikes
whiten the dunes
she now faces
over my shoulder.*

*Heat, rain, prickly green
hidden cottonmouths
lurking gators
the fecund flashes
of virgin Florida
the last patch
of unravaged seacoast
from Sandestin
to Panama City.*

*Julie's shocking blue eyes
peer up
from the face
of a Cambodian Buddha
like the ones
at Angkor Wat
before it was bombed.*

*Apple cheeks
perfect nose
eyelids like
curves of serenity
a smile to launch
a billion dreams.*

What's she hiding in there?

*She's not really
a blank slate
is she?*

*Genetic memory
to begin with.
Eons of evolution
coded in every cell.*

*And then the question
of Reincarnation
(Bodhisatva*

*can you help us
with this?)*

*If she's really lived
a thousand lives
then why, now
this baby charade?*

*Nine months already
of poopy diapers
and squirmy rebellion
infantile anti-climax
but oh
so delicious.*

She's here!

*She should be
writing
organizing
speaking
like she did
so many times
before
showing us the way
throwing the I Ching
handing out leaflets
inspiring the masses.*

*Why this Daddy-daughter dance
when we've been together
so many times
so many ways?*

*If you were
a Senator in Rome
a famous Socialist
or Queen What's-Her-Face
then why are you now*

*just resting in my arms
taking my breath away?*

*Speaking of which
thanks to our
polluter-destroyed
ozone-less sky
we're burnt to a crisp.*

*Panama hats
long-sleeve shirts
and sunscreen…
wasn't that
the corporate prescription
for a stricken planet
plummeting toward disaster?*

*Trillions in debt
and nothing to show
but ravaged cities
dead schools
barren wastelands
and ravenous corporations
ransacking
every nook
of your Mother's body.*

*Babes
we got our work cut out for us.*

*But then again
the state of Florida
broke though it is
has just bought
this piece of beach
and soon will erect a sign
"Nature Preserve."*

The turtles will

*continue to breed here
the lightening will strike
the rain will fall
the scrub trees will grow
and the bulldozers
won't come.*

*This chunk of planet
has been saved
and someday may
help save US.*

*Isn't that
why we do it?*

*Also
the Russian missiles are down
the SAC bombers
went off
Red Alert
two days
before you were born.*

Pretty good.

*We've won a few
we'll win some more.*

*It's in our genes
in our blood
this will to survive.*

*You're living proof
aren't you?
Just one
of the many reasons
that you came.*

*You can explain
them all
later
if you want to.*

You feel so perfect in my arms.

Part ONE:

TROPICAL DEPRESSION

The gray torrent
howls through Miami
through the beaches
through the glades
through the pools of my heart
and the deepest reaches of my loss
like a hurricane from Hell
a grim, grimy reaper
shredding my paltry defenses
mocking that thin painted wall
that faces the world
leaving me bare and embarrassed
saddened, confused
bleeding
lost.

Dad

*When last I was here
the Fountain failed us
youth so long gone.*

*I watched it pass for them
my beautiful parents
through middle age
when I first came back home to them
into the realm of the infirm
and the dying
the aches and pains
catching up with them
slowing them down
dissolving their sleepless nights
and foregone good times.*

How they loved to live.

*How I loved our luminous moments
of soul connection.*

*Complex lives
we all shared
often difficult,
always interesting
compelling
gorgeous
in their humanity.*

*He, my Dad, my beautiful Dad
so complex, so driven
but so loving and so simple.*

*Brilliant, rare,
magnetic, deeply loving
deeply loved.*

A little guy,
maybe five-five.

Nary a mean bone
not even a trace
though he could tease
especially me
because he knew
I could be vulnerable
so serious
so literal
such a perfect foil.

But he knew I was strong
could take it
grow from it
and maybe he was a bit jealous of that
so tortured
by manic depression
a chemical disorder
that struck him unawares
back in 1946
when I was
nine months old.

My mother took him
to doctor after doctor
for shock treatments
and drugs
while she held me
in the car
waiting with dread
not knowing who (or what) would return to her
from the bleak offices
of unfeeling quacks
who didn't really know
what they were doing
and maybe didn't care
all that much

*seeing my Dad
as an interesting subject
for further explorations
of an elegant puzzle.*

*He was a sly, graceful athlete
artistic, unpretentious
fifth of eight
in an old world family
in the Roxbury shtetl.*

*Street smart
raw ghetto male
full of vim
my Dad
loved me, his only son
beyond all measure
without bound
without reservation
without the slightest holding back
ever.*

He was warm.

He held me.

*How I must have howled
waiting in that car
while he howled inside
searching for answers
to an excruciating illness
we still don't understand
a half-century later.*

*But he kept it at bay
stood up to it.*

*What an incredible lifeforce
to survive those agonies*

to fight through those decades.

*Which was worse
the doctors
or the disease
the flashes of shock
or the depths of darkness?*

*To know him
outside the house
you'd've never known
he was a victim.*

*He loved to laugh
loved to make you laugh
always had a joke
always a smile
always a warm hug.*

*He was a third baseman without peer
flawless fielder
punch hitter
team player
great speed
cunning on the base paths.*

*I remember those few games
I covered him
from left
the two of us
in a line
on the ballfield.*

*Did I bat behind him?
send him around the bases
in front of me?*

*YES! I do remember
at Camp Willson*

*the YMCA paradise
in rural Ohio
where he took me
in 1969
with my hippie hair
and peacenik swagger
the war still raging
while the judges and Congressmen
wanted a lynching
right there on the pitchers mound.*

*When I blew one
over the fence
they called it foul.*

Bullshit.

*So I put
the next one out
and they all shut up.*

*Dad probably told that story
every day
for the rest of our lives
to anyone
who would listen
clerks
waitresses
salesmen
bridge partners who'd heard it
fifty times before
but loved him
and loved hearing it
yet again
and now would give
all they have
and might have been
to hear it one more time
from Sig's live lips.*

*How it hurts
to know he's gone.*

*My eyes well up
I cannot type.*

A Tropical Depression

The angry gale
batters the windows
of our tasteful hotel
with a pelting wet
beating the rhythms
of God's percussion.

We watch the palms
bend and sway
like fancy dancers
in a fertile shower.

This place reeks of sex
a pungent, delicious odor
of spreading legs
and sultry sensuality.

I love Miami
love this rain
as it thrusts its life force
in ceaseless pellets
against the glass
of this refurbished monument
to elegant decadence.

I'm down here
to visit close friends
they're working hard
at the end of a job.
I'm here to
ease them through
add some companionship
some side trips
a little stability
a little fun
some warm friendship
and support

at the end of a tour.

*But today I am
anything but stable.*

*The gray storm
pours in
through my eyes
and clouds my spirit.*

*It's way too dark
ten fathoms too deep
to lift my soul.*

*It oppresses
leaves me leaden
ungainly
confused.*

*I stop shaving
my clothes bag
I get underfoot
say the wrong things
cling.*

*Later I apologize
but I'm not too clear
about what for.*

*Something's wrong
I can feel it
but I can't say it
can't snap out of it
and can't pinpoint
where it's coming from.*

*A tropical depression
a disturbance in the force
a flood of repressed memories*

*sap my strength
snap my soul
like a matchstick shack
in a Caribbean twister
far too strong
to ride with words
until I escape
get some distance
lie ill for two weeks
safe and quiet
out of the rain
out of the gray
in the flat,
dry midwest
until the phrases
come.*

"Be a Big Person"

They were with me down there
my Mom and my Dad
just nine months prior.

It was for a convention
at one of those absurd
Collins Avenue hotels
gaudy and gauche
like 1950s flamingoes
dressed up for dinner
floor show by Jackie Gleason
Ike President
Elvis King.

Conspicuous consumption
white vinyl belts
toupees and beehives
red sport coats.

The convention is for their uniform business
a trade organization
they joined in the seventies
when first they went out
on their own
two little people
in an Ohio town
Nancy in college
me just out
a few shoes
a few thousand bucks
and an idea.

They were fifty-two years old.

It must have been
absolutely terrifying
at least for Mom.

*Dad probably
never gave it
a second thought
just went out
and fought
day after day
with that indomitable will
fought off his depressions
fought off the big guys
fought off the shysters
and never thought twice
kept to his principles
kept to his ethics
kept to his belief
that the customers
deserve it all
while Mom kept the books.*

*She wasn't much for clothes
not much for show.*

*She had a
simple, functional house
solid, functional cars.*

*Bored by the famous
and the rich
she embraced the people
whose minds could challenge her
whose principles she trusted
whose souls warmed her
whose children she liked.*

*They all called her
"a good person".*

*She hated the hypocrites
and would quietly say so
hated the bigots*

hated the petty.

"Be big," she always said.
"Be a big person."

The small stuff,
she would not tolerate.

Smallness of spirit
that could often abound
at these very conventions
where Mom and Dad dragged me
to learn their business
built from nothing
that they wanted to pass
to me and my sister
to the six grandkids
and maybe beyond.

Mom wasn't sure
that was such a great idea
but when push came to shove
she practically begged me
and it was she
that dragged me
off the commune
out of the country
away from the writer's alcove
and into the world
of shoes and uniforms
business and finance
and the bizarre hallucinogen
of Hallendale hotels

She was the essence of grace
all her days.

A stunning figure
when she was young

*shy but strong
a hidden zen
blessed in her quiet
as she aged
born,
like Dad,
a year and two miles
from JFK
sharing his vision
and his verve.*

*She exercised like a champ
deep into her seventies
until four years prior
to this rainstorm
walking the indoor track
or the summer sidewalks
while she talked with her friends
about the right to vote
and dumping at last
the latest crew
of mean-spirited thugs.*

*"The Almighty Buck," she said
"That's what it all boils down to."*

*In a way that made you
take her for granted
she kept an airy, sunny house
and my father solvent
garnering a circle
of thoughtful friends
who were fiercely loyal.*

*Unobtrusive as she was
they could not imagine
life without her.*

So when something struck her

*made her tired
made her fall down
took her off
the walking track
who could have guessed
it would finally take her
altogether
since the very thought
of Mom being gone
seemed to contradict
life itself.*

*She never complained
had no patience
for talk of illness
or illness itself.*

*When I first came back
I lived in their house
for two full years
with surprising comfort.*

*It was good to know them
at age 35
having fled with no sense
at age 17.*

*Now I found
I really liked them
would have been their friend
even if they
weren't my parents
(it might have been simpler).*

*What an incredible blessing
to have that.*

*Now I watched them traverse
that invisible barrier*

*between people who are
middle aged
can walk and drive
still play a little ball
still dance and cut loose—-
to people now old
putting away the
third baseman's mitt
flirting with a cane
talking about arthritis.*

It was sad to see.

*But most of the time
I didn't let it register
convinced myself
that they were really
just acting.*

*As soon as their spirits picked up
their bodies would rejuvenate
and Dad and I
would play ball again
while Mom and I
would resume our long walks
and pleasant talks.*

*But one night
she developed a nose bleed.*

"Parts wear out," she said.

*She'd see the doctor
after the weekend.*

*But the blood gushed
at one am
Dad yelled up
their bedroom awash*

*in sticky red
Mom on the toilet
in her nightgown
barely conscious
mumbling incoherent.*

*I pulled her off
dragged her across the room
put her legs up on the bed
and covered her
and threw cold water
on her face
while Dad called 911.*

*As she revived
she said she was ok
"it's enough already
let me up."*

*They took her to the hospital
she'd lost
half the blood
in her body
it took seven hours
to stop the flow.*

*Now something terrible
was eating her alive
making her weak
stopping her walks
which weakened her further
while she said nothing.*

Lose Phyllis?...not conceivable

Dolphins Plus

Years ago
these bent palms
were bathed in sunshine

We escaped the Fountainbleu
with its blasting AC
and lights always on
every aisle
every room
every lobby
every patio
a blazing meat locker
slab concrete
and nuclear power
in a war to the death
against tropical green.

Energy crisis? WHAT energy crisis?

We scooted our rent-a-car
past Turkey Point
(South Florida's aptly named
double-nuke;
watch it glow
when the next hurricane hits)
down to Key Largo
Bogie and Bacall
and a neat little place
where you swim with dolphins.

I'd been there before
despite eco-doubts
about such things
I like this place
this Dolphins Plus
they save beached sharks

*and do their best
to keep the faith.*

*So I told Mom and Dad
"come with me
watch me swim
with amazing animals."*

*Dad paused
turned up his nose
"if I can't swim
I'm not going."*

It hadn't occurred to me.

He WAS seventy-two years old.

*But sure
what the hell.*

*Together we swam
back and forth
pushing kickboards
to create a wake
that might entice
the surfing creatures
to pay us a visit
look us in the eye
favor us with some attention.*

*And there we were
me and my Dad
the guy who taught me
how to swim
when I was four
in the towering waves
at Nantasket Beach.*

*Now
two thousand miles south
we held hands as we kicked
back and forth
fifty yards
across a pond
where gorgeous space creatures
rode our father-son wake
smiling surfers
lending cosmic grace
to our ageless
primal bond.*

*The next day
under a pleasant February sun
we hit the glades
flat green river of grass
Shark Valley National Park
two seven-mile strips
of narrow slab
into the realm
of gators
and swamp deer.*

*They rode the tram
and fairly swooned
over the stunning beauty
of my sacred secret.*

*A joy to share it with them
what more could a son want?*

*Two years later
I want to do it again
"Let's do the glades!
let's do the dolphins!"*

*But now it's different.
The skies are gray
and my parents are failing*

*Dad's mind
is starting to wander
his memory
never exactly sharp
slumps to fuzz
his knees ache
baseball and handball
tennis and golf
are dimming snapshots*

Swim with the dolphins?

*"I'm awful tired, son.
Ask mother."*

*But mother
can barely walk.*

*"I'm so tired," she says
"I just don't understand.
I just can't believe it
All I want to do
is go back to bed."*

*I camp in a flophouse
down the beach
commuting up
to the palace
of the death
about to claim those
who gave me birth.*

*Days later
Mom has a heart attack
not a big one*

*just enough
to put her in the hospital.*

*She's too weak for the balloon
and that long-festering blood disease
for which she's refused
to take treatment
for nearly four years
then pneumonia
all sap her strength
prevent them
from opening her up
to clear out the artery
that feeds her heart.*

*Meanwhile Dad
begins to bounce
off the walls
like he did
that nosebleed night
she almost died.*

*He can barely cope
he goes out for drives
always a frightening prospect
now even worse
and comes back
to an empty house
lost
afraid
lonely
beyond all definition
of the word.*

*Nancy and I
take turns.*

*We are now the parents
of the parents that raised us.*

*I shuttle my kids
to the hospital
and their house
the one thing I know
can bring them pleasure
bring them escape
light their eyes
and fading lives.*

*My precious daughters
make them shine
with fleeting moments
of temporary transcendence.*

*All the pain
all the frustration
dissolve in the instant
my girls arrive.*

*It's the purest love
I've ever seen
or ever expect to.*

One midnight
I return
to Dad in pain
confused
hurt.

I rub his back for him
one of the few times
I've ever done that.

His skin is smooth
firm to the touch.

He's bought a wheelchair
a bad sign.

*Between the sciatica
and the arthritis
he just can't get around.*

*But he's always upbeat
beating the demons
once again
at their game.*

*Tonight it's rough
he's got a pain
in the chest.*

*We figure it's from
stretching those shoulder muscles
in the wheelchair.*

*But a few nights ago
I saw him in such
agony
it was hard to behold.*

*His legs were killing him
his back
his gums
and he was so desperately worried
about Mom in the hospital:*

*"Do you think she's coming back?
I'm afraid she's not coming back
Do you think she'll be home?"*

*I looked at him there
in such tragic pain
and silently asked
"Dad,
is it time?
Is it time for you to go
and escape all this?"*

*A few nights later
back in the house
like I was
ten years prior
when I first came back
back to their business
back to their home
back to their need
back to their arms
tonight we talk
til three in the morning.*

*I rub his back
I'm in a daze.*

*Something is happening
and I can't say it.*

*A gray haze
covers my mind
clouds my faculties
in numbed dread.*

*At four, I doze off
at five, I hear him yell.*

*The pains in his chest
they're way out of line
"Son, we'd better go to the hospital."*

*He gets sort of dressed
he links his arm
over mine.*

*I can feel it now
the texture of his skin
the weight on my forearm
the brown fullness of his hair
with no sign of bald.*

*We struggle out
to Mom's white
Honda sedan.*

*He leans against
the front hood
and expresses his shock
the detached shock of an athlete
surprised by the pain
of an unexpected injury.*

*"Whoah," he says,
"this really hurts.
I wonder what it is.
"Could I be having
a heart attack?"*

We can't fathom it.

*We tear through the quiet streets
of the pre-dawn morning
sprinting cross town
to Mt. Carmel West
where Mom fidgets upstairs
in the cardiac ward.*

*I wheel him in
to the Emergency Room
they put him on a bed
a nonchalant young doctor
a nice enough guy
gives an instant analysis.*

*No real problem
a mild heart attack
needs a balloon
an angioplasty
"just like his wife.
We'll watch him
over the weekend."*

*Everyone's relaxed
we're in safe haven
Dad is thrilled
to be back in the same building
safe
with his beloved Phyllis.*

*"Wait til she hears,"
he says with real joy.
"Wait til she sees me here."*

Gifts Beyond Rubies

*Ten years prior
I remember him saying
much the same thing
at the Fountainbleu pool.*

*It was my first time around
with these trade show conventions.*

*We swam together
in those warm Florida pools
made the pact
that would bring me home.*

*And then
wouldn't you know...
there was Susan*

*My warm
dark beauty
living nearby
brilliant and clear
loving and sweet
swayed my senses
who could know
she would be
steadfast and strong
gentle and kind
the perfect match
for a family in progress
a perfect soul mate
a gift beyond rubies
for a spirit in need.*

*And before you could say
"come in the business"
there they were
the best possible joke*

*the cosmos can play
on an overdue father
TWINS
then another
three girls
plus another
Annie and Abbie, then Julie, and Rachel
four girls all together
(and Shoshanna yet to come)
with their fabulous mother
and lucky me
in a house just a mile
from Phyllis and Sig.*

Free at Last

*Those years of shared joy
and absolute happiness
now came to focus
in this one
crosstown hospital.*

*Mom on the fifth floor
Dad in the basement
now getting his first taste
of sister morphine.*

*I tell the attendants
he's in serious pain
his back hurts him
he can barely lie down
his knees are aflame
his chest a torment
is there anything
anything
to help?*

*The IVs are flowing
Dad looks hungrily
at a paramedic
"how about some pain killer?"
he asks
with the eager naiveté
of a virgin initiate
to some exotic cult*

*At home
his office
is cluttered with pills
and syringes
and the discomfiting array
of a very ill
but very powerful man*

*trying to treat himself
for too many ailments.*

*The insulin, the advil
the anti-depressants, the relaxants
the desperate pharmacy
of an amateur self-medicant
losing control
of his crumbling body.*

*Here in the hospital
his jumble of pain
eases onto a bed
where respite is hopeless
a lifeline is offered.*

"Yes," she says, "we can give you some morphine."

*The reaction is instant
I can see his mind settle
his body relax
his tensions ease
as he escapes pain
for the first time in days
in months
maybe in fact
for the first time really
in fifty years
since those awful Moments
when I howled in the car
as they searched for answers
that fifty years later
they may have just found
as the herbal concoction
flows through the tubes
and into his bloodstream
into his pain centers
maybe into his soul
beckoning him on*

*beckoning him elsewhere
beckoning him out
to the joy of his youth
the free float of the ocean
the love of his life.*

*For the first time ever
I see him totally free
free of the pain
free of the doubt
floating on air
completely content.*

*It's Friday morning
we're set for the weekend
"The timing is perfect,"
says the young doctor.
"He'll rest til Monday
maybe til Tuesday
we'll run all the tests
then do the balloon.
It seems it's the same artery
that's blocked in his wife."*

Dad likes that.

He's here with Phyllis.

*He can't wait to see her
can't wait to tell her
about this amazing coincidence.*

*They wheel him up
to the third floor
(she's on the fifth)
a nice big room
nicer than Mom's
lots of equipment
busy nurses*

*in and out
running tests
making him comfortable.*

*He loves the attention
loves the company
loves the audience.*

*He jokes with them
laughs
tells his favorite stories.*

*I've run back home
grabbed some things
books
clothes
his box of insulin.*

*driving back to the hospital
the sun is rising
all pinks and golds
there's a peaceful feeling
things are going to be
alright.*

*I bring him his books
his clothes
his medicines
now extraneous
given he's in
an actual hospital.*

*We talk for a bit
he's really ecstatic
I'm barely awake
with my one hour's sleep.*

*"Look," he jokes to a nurse,
"He can't keep his head up."*

*I smile
and try to decide:
should I go home to sleep
or to the pool to swim?*

*Then I remember
a guy from a shoe company
is coming to the store.*

*I could blow it off
but given my stupor
it's as good an option as any.*

*Now I know
what I should have done
was go upstairs
wake up Mom
and bring her down
to say hi to Dad
one last time.*

*Back at the office
we're wheeling and dealing.*

*The small paneled office
the captain's quarters
of Dad's little ship
walled with pictures
of the family
and the awards
of a fifty-year career.*

*I've been in here
for two weeks now
since Dad stopped coming
an amazing turn
Mom said:*

*"I never thought I'd see the day
when Sig would not
go into that office."
That business was his child
his playground
his ego his obsession.*

*He loved it
loved being there
loved running it
touching it
walking down the aisles
making notes for improvements
joking with the help
taking pride in his accomplishment.*

*It was a beautiful creation
for him and Mom
supporting three families
he loved to say
the others in the field
called him a giant
having started from nothing
and transformed
an entire industry.*

*Before Sig Wasserman
came on the scene
dealers selling
uniforms and shoes
to postal workers
often treated them
like army privates
at the quartermaster counter.*

*Dad pampered them
like true friends
took back anything
they didn't like*

and bragged about it.

*They loved him
loved what he did for them
loved how he respected them
and forced the rest of the industry
to do the same*

*He was, in his way,
a real revolutionary
fighting the Big Guys
the way we fought the Pentagon
to end that damn war.*

*He always supported me
in those efforts
and when I came
back to Columbus
and saw what he
really did
I was equally proud.*

*We did have our fights
mostly about computers
which he understood
a shade less than I.*

*We also argued
over finance and strategy
he liked to pick fights
from time to time
to test the limits
and my mettle.*

*But by and large
for ten full years
we got along
grew together
activist and businessman*

*Mom keeping the books
Nancy selling gifts
somehow
it worked.*

*Today
the shoe guys
are offering
such a deal
a special buy-out
a hot number discontinued.*

*I'm a little groggy
so Dad's friend Marty
our capable store manager
does the purchase
we take quite a few pair
at a pretty good price*

*Later,
the Big Guy screws us
delivers the bad sizes
the sixes and sevens
twelves and thirteens
but the ones that really sell
the eights through elevens
they pull out of the shipments
and sell to someone else
for an extra buck or two
leaving us empty-handed
and our customers angry.*

*It's just the kind of duplicity
Dad hated beyond measure.*

*In all the years I knew him
I never once heard
anyone
question my father's*

*ethics or honesty
openness or compassion.*

*What more can one say
about a man?*

He Releases Us

While I sit in his captain's chair
the phone rings.

My heart sinks:
"Is it Mom or is it Dad?"

"It's your father."

As we arrive
Nancy and I
they are pumping his heart.

One of the orderlies
makes a crack
about whether they're going to
"jump on the corpse"
all day long.

I suppose
it's as good a way
as any
to hear
your father
is dead.

My sister and I
burst into tears
involuntary
surprising.

How could he go?

The void just doesn't register.

He lies there
in bed

tubes coming out
every which way
eyes closed
unshaven
just a few short hours ago
so pitifully in pain
then thankfully released
now on the tail end
of some kind
of transition.

I hope it was good for him.

I hope it was right.

They remove the tubes.

When last I left
they'd prevented me
from kissing his face
so I'd kissed his hand instead

Now I touch him
kiss his whiskers
but the heat is going
he's no longer warm
he's no longer there.

He really is
no longer alive.

The shock sets in
it's hard to navigate
between
the reality of the hospital room
its sounds
its smells
its people
living lives
doing work.

*Their father
has not just died.*

*Their world
is somewhere else.*

*And us
my sister and I
the reality before us
our very best
most loyal friend
lying there
or at least his body
lifeless
over.*

*Do we call the rabbi?
do we tear our clothing?
do we embrace the body?
do we pace the room?*

*Eventually
they all come
Susan, the kids
the rabbi
the friends.*

Arrangements are made.

*I hold Dad's hand
as long as I can
linger
while the attendants
wait
to take him to the funeral home.*

*Finally
grudgingly
there's a comfort.
What do I feel?*

What do I know?

Nothing.

*He's gone
his pain is over
the platitudes rush in*

*"He's happier where he's gone"
all that stuff.*

Meaningless

*Dad' is just not there
anymore.*

*That's his body
but its lifeforce
is gone
that's it.*

*Finally
I let go
his hands are cool
they're still his
but it's different
they grant me a sense
that this moment is over.*

*He releases us
and they take him away.*

"Go to the Light"

*For three full nights
Dad's body lay
in the funeral home.*

*Under orthodox Jewish law
a funeral cannot be held
on the Shabbos
and he has chosen to go
on a Friday morning,*

*The rabbi says
that's auspicious
the sign
of a real holy man
especially on the weekend
of Tu'be Sh'vot
a holiday of real joy
and true liberation.*

*A funeral
before the day is over
is impossible.*

*Saturday is out.
Sunday's too quick.*

*We want to give the Boston family
and all his business buddies
time to get here.*

So Monday it will be.

*But under orthodox Jewish law
the body
of the recently deceased
cannot be left
alone.*

*Until it is buried
it must be accompanied
at all times.*

*Usually
the funeral home
takes care
of such things.*

*But it's Shabbos
no one's available
until Saturday night.*

*So Nancy and her husband Phil,
Susan and I
take turns
running shifts and shuttles
back and forth
between our nearby homes
and our warm loving children
and the body of our Dad
lying in state
on a chill metal table
in an unheated room
in the back of a funeral home
with a candle and a phone
covered with a white sheet.*

*So the hours passed
in a chill April blur
the cruelest month.*

*Back at the hospital
as he lay there
and they removed the tubes
a bright young nurse
said he was doing
just great
laughing and joking*

*and then she asked us
"Did he speak Yiddish?"
"Yes," said Nancy, "yes he did."*

*The nurse then explained
that all of a sudden
he started speaking to her
in a language
she didn't understand
and then
it hit
a heart attack
of massive proportion
that instantly
effortlessly
put him under.*

*The nurse wondered
what he'd been saying
he was such a nice man
so friendly and bright
as was she.*

*Mom later guessed
he was saying the Sh'ma
the essential Hebrew prayer
"Hear O Israel
the Lord Our God
the Lord is One."*

*Tonight
as he lies here
his body graying
before my eyes
I call Diane
my mystic friend
healer and Empress.
He seems uneasy
he seems caught
he seems still there.*

*I can feel his life force
through his graying body
in the sad,
still quiet
of this backroom purgatory.*

*He seems to want out
there's something incomplete.*

*"Tell him," Diane says,
"to go to the Light.
Tell him to follow the Light."*

*In my left pocket
is a small stone
deep tan in color
carved with sanskrit
"Om Mane Padme Om".*

*I finger it
put it on his table
adjusting my yarmulke
as I do.*

*My hand
goes to his heart
his body is cooling
his skin is greying
athlete no more
lover no more
but always my father
forever my father
now maybe a spirit
getting free.*

*I point to the candle
and chant the mantra
"Go to the light, Dad,
go to the light."*

*Minutes or hours
I do not remember
but at some point
I felt a change.*

Imagined?

*Conjured up in the mind
of a saddened,
lost son?*

I don't know.

*But at some point
I felt it
a certain release
I hope it was him
going to the light
but feel it I did
a lightening of spirit
a delicate departure
a Divine breeze.*

*I left the room
then came back
his body was there
but he was gone.*

Dolphin Queen

*In the eye of the storm
we made a dash
back to the Dolphins
and Key Largo.*

*We knew it would pour
but who would care
we'd be in the water
and the prospect
of another visit
with these amazing beasts
was too much to pass up.*

It was a good gamble.

*The moment my friend
sticks her feet
in the water
two sleek females
jump right on her.*

*I have been here
a half-dozen times
and never seen
anything like it.*

*As she eases
into the pool
they gang up
to embrace her
push her around,
smother her
in dolphin delight.*

Me?
they could care less
so I submerge
swim with my back
to the bottom
about six feet down
and look up
as the silken silhouettes
of one great woman
and many powerful
cosmic fish
cavort and play
on the surface.

A sight to behold.

It's convincing confirmation
of what many of us
have long suspected
that our
red-headed friend
has mystic powers
of serious proportion.

Finally the chill
gets to her
at the break
she retreats
and I try
another pool
with four females
and one small baby boy
about four feet long
clinging to his Mom
as they swim
at amazing speeds
in perfect syncopation.

*But the day is dimming
a storm barrels in
as I search for air
it starts to pour.*

*I keep diving
as long as they let me
but the visibility
is no more.*

*This is the pool
where Dad and I swam
four years before
while Mom watched on
under the sun.*

That was a happy day.

This one's a challenge.

*We retreat to the restaurant
the Italian Fisherman
where my parents
watched the sunset
and fed the catfish
that swarm in the cove
beside our table.*

*The image of family
a perfect memory.*

*But today
the storm lashes
at shut glass doors
batters the boats
out at anchor
pours down chill
powerful torrents.*

*We've done the right thing
resting here
it's too dangerous to drive
we need to eat
and get warm.*

*But the pasta's oily
the energy raw.*

*Florida feels tormented
angry
as if it knows
what's in store.*

*the cosmos decided
that what we all
really needed
was to have our teeth
drilled
and our heads
battered
against a wall.*

*Mom came home
two days after
Dad died
put herself through
the entire ordeal.*

*When he first departed
that Friday morning
she hadn't seen him
didn't know
he was there.*

*We didn't know
how to tell her
what had happened.*

*So Nancy and I
and the bright young doctor
did it
in two stages.*

*First we asked
how she was
then gently informed her
that Dad had come
to the hospital
with a mild heart attack.*

*Then we left
acted as if
things were fine.*

*Then we came back
and told her
he just hadn't made it
had unexpectedly
passed away.*

*The first thing she said
"I didn't get
to say goodbye."*

*Then she went on
about how
maybe it was best
maybe it was
a good way to go
maybe he was
out of pain
at last.*

*But she kept coming back
to that one thing:
"I didn't get
to say goodbye.
Fifty years
I didn't even get
to say goodbye."*

*In droves they came
to the house
the family, the friends
the rabbi, the minions
I went to shul
early each morning
to say Kaddish
then they came*

*to the house
in the evening.*

It was torture.

*It exhausted Mom
wore her down
she kept saying
how much Dad
would have loved it
the food
the friends
the conversation
the endless stream
of warm, loving people.*

*By week's end
she could barely stand.*

*Soon thereafter
she got strong enough
to do the balloon.*

*She went back
to the hospital
where Dad passed away
and they opened the artery
that had denied her heart
the blood it needed.*

*We all figured
this would do it
her heart would strengthen
her verve would return
and Phyllis could be Phyllis.*

*But things went
the other way
she came home
from the hospital
and all she could say was:
"I can't do anything but sleep"
"I didn't even get to say goodbye."*

*Her mind was sharp
but her spirit was bent
her body was broken.*

A rain of toxic death

*Early on
to escape the madness
I took Annie and Abbie
back to Dad's gravesite.*

*A few people
had sent flowers
not the Jewish custom
but we made use of them.*

*We planted them all
on my father's grave
the earth still open
after the digging.*

*We turned it to
a strawberry field
an absurd collage
of colors and blooms.*

*If the gravesites were people
Dad's was the hippie.*

*It was fun to do
but I felt uneasy
in that cemetery
just four miles
directly downwind
from central Ohio's
trash burning power plant
just recently fingered
as the nation's
very worst emitter
of lethal dioxin.*

*The burner opened
in 1983*

*just as I came
back to Columbus.*

*It was not something
we paid much heed
it seemed a good
green idea
burning the trash
to get the energy
while reducing the waste stream.*

*But in January
I got a phone call.*

*For twenty years
I'd been traveling
all over the world
fighting nuclear plants
worried (among other things)
about radioactive fallout
nuclear terrorism
melt-downs
and worse.*

*Now a co-conspirator
wanted to tell me
this trash burning power plant
was raining down death
on my very home town.*

What?

*Another industrial killer
on the prowl?*

*Another
homework assignment
in toxic pollution?*

*Soon after Dad's passing
I interviewed some people
living directly downwind
who did health surveys
of their own
soon confirmed
by the city and state
doubled rates
of cancer and heart disease.*

*The burner's owners
said it was due
to smoking and other
"life style decisions."*

*The people downwind
said it came
from vile black ash
laden with dioxin
cadmium, arsenic, mercury, bismuth, and lead
that rained down on them
and their children
most cloudy nights
and with every drizzle.*

*At Dad's funeral
I vowed
to do what I could
to help shut it
this good idea
gone wrong
just four miles upwind
from where he'd be buried.*

*And now my Mom
fading
in front of our eyes.*

Could it be the dioxin?

*After the melt-down
at Three Mile Island
I spent two years
interviewing countless women
just like my mother
who'd lost their health
their husbands, their children
to the radioactive fallout
from atomic testing.*

*Mormon women
conservative
patriotic
who couldn't believe
their government would ever
lie to them.*

But it did.

And now they knew it.

*So I co-wrote a book
called KILLING OUR OWN*

*The only way
to survive the task
was too keep
some distance
some "objectivity"
and insulate ourselves
from the emotion
of the tragedies
we were documenting.*

*But now I was watching
my own mother go.*

Could it be from the trash burner?

Could I ever get proof?

*We just didn't know
what was happening to her.*

*Her heart seemed to respond
but her blood disease worsened
she had no energy
just wanted to sleep.*

*We had our long talks
I brought her my kids
she told me what she wanted done
with the estate.*

*But she still couldn't believe
any of this
was happening to her.*

*"My world has turned
upside down.*

*"Except for having
you and Nancy
I've never set foot
in any hospital"
(she forgot about the nosebleed).*

She had no patience for it.

*We took her to a park
she could barely walk.*

*I kept wanting
to bring her the kids
she began saying
she was too tired.*

Finally

*they told us
what we already suspected.*

Lymphoma.

Cancer.

*Chemotherapy a possibility
if she gets strong
if it hasn't spread too far.*

*"My world
tuned upside down"*

*It had all seemed
to have gone to plan.*

*She'd wanted to travel
but Dad hadn't.*

*We all knew
if she went first
he'd never make it.*

*Now he was gone
and she was ready
to kick up her heels
be the merry widow
with so many
of her girlfriends
also widowed.*

*But there it was
the C-word
turning her world
upside down
breaking her body
chipping away
at her spirit.*

*Was Dad up there
shouting
"Hey, Phyllis
it's GREAT here
you gotta see this
come on
come back to me"?*

Was that what was going on?

*I wanted her
to see the world
see Paris
Bangkok
Beijing and Bali
the whole world beckoned
there was nothing
holding her back.*

*Nothing
but a deadly disease
draining her strength
killing her body
and all those good times
for which we'd all waited
so very long.*

*Was it a random molecule
she had breathed
a few years ago
when out at the cemetery
for someone else's funeral?*

*Or maybe cadmium
lodged on some lettuce
or a dual assault
by chlorine and lead.*

*So many people
who'd lost their children
lost their mothers
lost their lives
to industrial disease
concealed forever
by smug bureaucrats
and cynical investors.*

*Now there she was
my very own mother
being eaten alive
by a polluted curse.*

*All through that summer
we fought the inevitable
Nancy and me
hanging on
to our parents
and all their dreams.*

*Nancy the artist
soul mate to my father
at one with his spirit
how she could stand
this psychic assault
was truly a testament
to the strength
of her soul.*

Now Mom was sinking.

*Again we played parent
to our beautiful child
the one who gave us birth
slipping out of our grasp.*

*Back and forth
to the hospitals*

*she hated every minute
but what could she do?*

*Hour after hour
she lolled in her bed
wondering why
it had all
come to this.*

*We rubbed her feet,
which she loved.*

*It was a joy for me
to see her get
such pleasure
like rubbing Dad's back
that very last
heart-breaking day.*

*Finally one night
one Saturday night
Susan and I
went to visit.*

*It was quiet
and dark
well after hours
we spoke softly with Mom
about family issues
and what would come next
and how we all loved her.*

*I rubbed her feet
she seemed ecstatic.*

We hugged her.

We kissed her

Then we left her.

*We went to the movies:
"Little Buddha"
about dying
transmigration of the soul
precisely everything
we needed to see.*

*Next morning
Nancy called
"come right away."*

*Mom was going
into fits.*

*She'd lost contact
her body was flailing
the battle had turned.*

*They put her in
intensive care
and we debated
what her will said
about being
kept alive.*

*A few more weeks
going as she was
she did not want.*

*She was leaving
but how? but when?*

*They did what they could
short of measures
that would keep her alive
in a vegetative state.*

*Intensive care
but not life support.*

*Her brother and sister
rushed out from Boston.*

*She seemed
occasionally aware
acknowledged them each
but could not put
five words together.*

*We told her we loved her
we embraced her as often
as much as we could
till finally she said
clearly and distinctly
"it's enough already."*

Two days stumbled on.

*We sat through the nights
watching her fidget
uncomfortably
through the long
quiet hours
of darkness
and pain
looking for
a Moment's peace
a Moment's communication.*

*Finally
on Tuesday
I talked to her
told her everything
I needed to say.*

"Thank you, dear," she said.

82

That was the last I heard.

*On Wednesday
she ceased thrashing
gradually
her body
calmed itself
loaded with pain killers
and morphine
like Dad
she slowed
her functions
hit a rhythm
peaceful enough.*

*We all had our cries
alone and together
and soon we all came
to a level of peace
so fitting for Mom
as if she'd planned it that way
set out a transition period
for her impending departure
so we could all adjust
and fall into acceptance.*

*All those places she could have gone
all those things she could have done
the seminars
the elderhostels
the mountains
the reefs
foregone
for now
till some other lifetime
in some other body
some other circumstance.*

How we would miss her.

Amazing Grace

*In those four days
from Sunday to Thursday
we lived it all
adjusted
prepared
to accept her going
with the grace of her living.*

*They moved her
out of intensive care
to a room high up
at the end of a hall
all to her own
set specially aside
for precisely this purpose.*

*Through Wednesday and Thursday
her bodily functions
gradually slowed.*

*She was comfortable
she breathed quietly
more slowly.*

*I spent
all day Thursday
committed for the duration
with sleeping bags and a pillow
making a life
in the place right beside her
holding her hand
counting her breaths.*

*I brought in a boom box
and organic provisions.
Nancy too*

*making a life here
as Mom faded
breathing slower
and slower.*

*Just past eleven
we were each
holding a hand.*

*Nancy said
"How about some music?"*

*When we were kids
Mom had two records
Beethoven's Sixth Symphony
Rachmaninoff's Third Piano Concerto.*

*She played them constantly
implanting the power
of classical music
deep into our souls.*

*So now it's Beethoven's Second
the music I played
in the operating room
when the twins were born
seven years prior.*

*I punched the button
the music came on.*

*I turned back
picked up her hand
within an instant
her breathing stopped.*

She just stopped.

She just left.

*It was 11:20
the exact time of night
our twins
were born.*

*And now
Grandma was gone
my mother was gone
my sister and I
totally orphaned
strange though it sounded
to parents
of six kids
now there was
no one
between us
and the void
no Mom
no Dad
to hug
to hold
to fend off the future
to be that buffer
between now
and what comes next.*

Twins in passing

*An hour later
we were back
at that funeral home
Mom and me
back in that room
on that cold metal table
where Dad had departed
four months ago.*

*This time
it was different
Mom wasn't there
didn't make the journey
from the hospital.*

She'd already left.

Her body was empty.

*There was no need to talk
about "going to the light."*

It was "enough already."

*No need to meditate
or to mourn
on her account.*

*By late afternoon
she was down
in the ground
beside Sig
in a much cheaper coffin.*

*She'd wanted to donate
her body to science*

*but she was too old
and too riddled
with all those diseases.*

*So in her spirit
on the spur of the moment
I saved a thousand bucks
on a simple pine box
which we'll give to the doctors
for further research.*

*It worked out fine
because in the orthodox religion
you can't cut up the body
and still be admitted
to the cemetery.*

*This way
she makes the donation
and still gets buried
next to Sig.*

*This time
no sitting shivve.*

*After the funeral
we all had a dinner
back at the house
around the warm table
the dark, pecan table
they brought with Boston
a half-century ago
glowing still
with all the beautiful dinners
my Mom had made us
over the years
all the Friday nights
all the holidays
all the celebrations*

*on that sweet
deep brown table
laden with food
made by her hand
and her heart.*

*No one will ever
match what she did
who she was
how we loved her.*

*I sat in Dad's seat
mournfully presiding
with her brothers and sister
family and friends
over the last of these dinners
the tears of our longing
the tears of our joy
the tears of our blessing
the tears of our loss
spicing the meal
and all we felt.*

*The next day
Saturday
everyone fled
back to Boston
to her brother's
80th birthday
rather than sit
a stationary target
for another round
of mournful group torture.*

*I stayed behind
went to their room
lay on their bed
till deep in the night
I felt their presence*

*their love
all they'd given me
life itself
their hands on my back
their souls in my bloodstream.*

Forever.

Twins in rebirth

Back in Miami
the job is done
my days as the bull
in my friends' china shop
have come to an end
at least for now.

Us earnest types
we can always manage
to step on a few toes
with the best of intentions
when the moment is wrong.

It's time to go
back to the northland.

It's been a horrible year
not only my Mom
not only my Dad
but Andrea Simon
eighty-six years old
a Mum to me
when Mom wasn't around
and from September on
as election day neared
the progressive and good hearted
dying in droves
people we loved
people we needed
Andy Kopkind
Raoul Julia
Burt Lancaster
Jerry Rubin
Erwin Knoll

*Shlomo Carlebach
the singing rabbi
who married us
in song and spirit.*

*They just seemed to fall
one after the other
as if the grim reaper
had gone to the left
grabbing all he could
to guarantee
the election of 1994
the Gingrich putsch
of the petty and mean
would carry with it
the sting and the stigma
of physical death
to lend credence and pain
to the spiritual demise
of a nation in decline.*

My father's joy, my mother's peace

*Amidst the turmoil
it finally all
made perfect sense
going back to Ohio
back to my parents
back to my hometown
which is after all
a parent too
and needs to be understood
needs to be loved
before one can move on.*

*Old as I was
with illusions of having
"been around"
I still had not known
the amazing people
who gave me birth
and raised me
from whom I had
youthfully fled
before we could really
get acquainted.*

*A good thing I came back
no matter what
it seemed to cost
because now they're gone
but know them I did.*

*This Florida storm
has struck back
unseasonable
unreasonable
way too harsh
wrecking crops*

*flooding the Everglades
exposing the swamp deer
to ravaging gators.*

*The path in Shark Valley
is deep under water
the parents I took there
are deep under ground.*

*The mobbed plane
barely gets us out
like the last refugees
off that Saigon roof.*

*Above the clouds
the sun is shining.*

*When I finally get home
to Susan and the kids
my Rachel
my twins
my Julie
my sun
to the house that still sits
a mile from my parents'
a mile from my sister's
my girls are all doing
what children will do
at sixteen and seven,
seven and three.*

*They romp around the house
yell and fight
tickle each other
and love their Daddy.*

*I am ill
and worn out
though I've been gone
just five days.*

*Being away
has dropped my defenses
opened me up
to the power of mourning.*

*For weeks I'm immobile
sick and feeble
the days pass
doing nothing.*

I visit my parents' house.

*Sometimes they're there
sometimes they're not.*

*I see the old men
at the health club
every few days
my heart leaps:
"Hey! Dad!"*

But it's not him.

*And Mom's not calling
about the girls
talking gently
soothing
knowing.*

How I long for that voice.

*But Susan's here
and our girls.*

We laugh and we joke
I tickle them
they yell
play horsey
tickle me back
and the healing progresses.

I am now to them
what my folks were to me
the line of defense
the cushion of safety
between now and the future
the protecting presence
the unquestioning love.

I cannot imagine
what it would have been like
to lose my parents
without kids
of my own
to hug and to hold
to cherish and balance.

My heart opens to anyone
who goes through this
alone.

It is an ordeal
I can't fathom.

Tonight
as usual
I read to the twins
each on a shoulder
Julie on my tummy
Rachel listening
we read the stories
Beethoven on the boom box
I say the Kaddish:

"Yisgadal v'yiskadah sh'may raboh."
And then we all say the Shema:
"Shemah Yisroael Adonoi Elohanu Adonoi Echad."

Then they say their prayers
asking Ha'Shem to help them
not pee in their bed
asking that Gramma and Grampa
be happy and healthy
safe and warm.

And then
they doze off.

I listen to them breathe
feel their beating hearts
surrounding me
with heat and love
comfort and life.

And soon
amidst the memories
amidst the overwhelming power
of the almighty present
there comes the taste
the exquisite gift

of my father's joy
and my mother's peace.

Part TWO:

A GLIMPSE OF THE BIG LIGHT

*The water
in the JCC Pool
is way too hot
close to ninety
maybe more.*

*They've raised it
for the elders
with their aches
and arthritis
and for the kids
still too little
to take the cold.*

*For those of us
who swim long distances
it becomes a challenge
to stay awake.*

*After the first
mile or two
you begin to feel
like a lobster
with a boiled brain.*

*But today the heat
has its benefits.*

*I've been swimming
for about an hour
sixty-four laps
to the mile.
I'm at just over a hundred
with another set
yet to go
on my usual route
Tuesdays and Thursdays
when the pool is emptiest
quiet*

and most peaceful.

*It's just a few months
since Dad and Mom
passed away.*

*Just a few days
since a tough meditation
at their house.*

*To forget
and to seek
I swim this pool
for hours at a time.*

*My Dad did it
a Boston polar bear
frigid Atlantic plunger
somehow
he could look
at this hot
heavily chlorinated
Ohio pool
and see the ocean.*

*Now that he's gone
this big blue box
looks to me
like a zendo.*

*Two hundred and sixteen laps
just over three miles
just over two hours.*

*I count them
in mantras of eighteen.*

An aerobic meditation.

A spiritual workout.

*Eighteen stands
for the Hebrew letters
symbolizing G-d.*

*Six 18s
make 108
a holy number
for Jews
and Buddhists*

*Since I
aspire to both
I do two.*

*My miles become
prayer wheels
my laps
like beads
on a bracelet:*

*108 beads
on a rosary.*

*108 stitches
on a baseball.*

*Three "Chai's" and a ten
make sixty four
that's a mile.*

*Ten "Chai's" make 180
plus twelve laps
make three miles.*

*Add eight laps
that makes two hundred.*

Then another sixteen
216
we are done.

Push hard
I'll do those two
108s
one for Dad
one for Mom
a watery yahrtzeit
an aerobic benediction.

I go on like this
my body
my brain
my soul
all approaching
the heat
and consistency
of deep-fried tofu
when

SUDDENLY

the White Light

HITS!

As I turn
in the deep end
at lap 107
nearing
"Chai" number six
the first 108
I am lost
in the count
trying to figure
how many miles
I've swum

*or will swim
when a voice shouts out
(in English)
"six laps, twelve miles
a hundred chais,
a thousand monkeys
what the hell difference
does it make?"*

*My mind caves
and explodes.*

HAH!!!

*Who cares
if I swim
100 laps
or a thousand?*

*What if they make
two miles
or ten?*

*I'm just going
back and forth
in a silly box
filled with water
seeing below
an endless
black
line.*

*What's it matter
if I swim
108
or not a one?*

*The jumble of my mind
lost in the count*

SUDDENLY

*it's gone!
consumed
obliterated
in White Light.*

*My mind
my body
whatever else
consists of me
becomes
a weightless
NOTHING
a vessel of bright…*

YES!!!

*I've read about this
a brush with the Zen
a beam from Ha'Shem
a flash of what's*

OUT THERE!

I am hilarious.

*The peace
the loss
the void
the liberation*

WOW!

*I am
somewhere
someone
ELSE!!*

*Unfortunately
(not that it really matters)
I am also
at the deep end
lost in the rapture
but not into drowning.

Hmmmm…
A contradiction?

I navigate
gingerly
on my back
to the shallows
finishing
as I go
lap 108
and sit
in
stunned
ecstatic
silence
while
WHITE LIGHT
runs through
my brain
body
what?…

Weightless
timeless
thoughtless
almost.

I am holding on
(or NOT holding on)
to this feeling of
pure
peace*

and
joy
while sitting in
a community swimming pool
in central Ohio
at the center
of my universe.

A Fool's Graduation

*The sun pours
through west facing windows.*

*This seems the end
of a long
long journey.*

*And a commencement
a confirmation
of a realm of experience
I've studied
dreamed
dissected
craved
and sometimes sought
but always…*

*I feel
incredibly peaceful
perfectly whole…*

SO I LAUGH!!!!

What a fool I am!

What a fool I'll BE!!!

*What has come
is pure
PROOF
(POOF!)
that on one level
one profound
cosmic
wonderful
amazing
plateau*

it really doesn't matter
what I do
what I don't
who I am
who I'm not…

Enough already!!!

We ease down
me
my body
my brain
my spirit
my soul
my my
all those various
currently ecstatic
components
of who
or what
ever
is writing this
experiencing THAT
and we RELAX
(all of us)
and ENJOY
savor
explore
until the cosmos
will somehow say
it's time
to leave
or swim again.

And in that time
that glorious interlude
those uncounted Moments
of pure
ecstatic

*gratification
we FEEL
what we've sensed
or known
or hoped
for a long
long time
that there IS
another level
another realm
of consciousness
and peace
beyond the LSD
hallucinations
and the herb-induced
glimpses
through the doors
of natural perception.*

*This seems more
like a quick dip
a meteoric plunge
holistic and blinding
shocking and benign
into the realm
of...*

WHAT?

*Way back when
all through the sixties
and the seventies
we tried to get here
tried to experience
something like this.*

*We were
amateur
(VERY amateur)*

*cosmic seekers
come out of the peace movement
and civil rights
back to the land
seeking spirit.*

*We fought nuke power
a holistic campaign
for the global environment*

*Those of us born
to genetic optimism
have ultimate faith
in the survival instincts
of our species
the renewable powers
of Mother Nature.*

*All through that era
the horrors
of injustice
and war
still reeling
from JFK's
unsolved murder
LBJ's
tragic betrayal
and Richard Nixon's
pitiful psychosis
we kept to that compass
that ultimate faith
in a benign outcome
a nurturing universe
a White Light
toward which
we crawled.*

*We hoped
and believed*

*if we fought hard
campaigned in good faith
never let go
sooner or later
all would be well.*

*We would not
incinerate our earth
in a nuclear Armageddon
even if Revelations
said we would.*

*The polluted whimper
the slow death
of global-warmed
eco-suicide…
well, hell
we could beat
even that.*

*Demonstrate!
Organize!
Meditate!
Empathize!*

*With solar energy
sustainable economics
common sense
our beloved planet
could become
a tangible paradise
our Mother Earth
would be respected
revered
embraced
bathed
at last
in White Light.*

*Through amazing times
and all those herbs
marijuana
mescalito
LSD...
and all those books
Carlos Castenada
BE HERE NOW
Baba Ram Dass
THIS IS IT
Martin Luther King
BIRMINGHAM JAIL
we came to believe
there was indeed
a level of consciousness
far beyond
what we saw.*

*We KNEW somehow
as an internal
nagging unease
 egged us on
that the universe
had to be
more than round
that the cosmos promised
something ELSE.*

*So
we searched.*

*We pestered mystics
like Elwood Babbitt
trance medium
backwoods farmer
Luckies addict
who used his body
as a "telephone"
for the spirits.*

Christ
Buddha
Einstein
Marshall Bloom
they all spoke
of a realm
not "up there"
but "out there"
said "Mark Twain"
whose spirit explained
patiently
wryly
that the news
of his demise
was STILL
premature.

Then the Maharishi
that simple mantra
chanting diligently
180 days
then it was time
to do something else
(though I could start again
at any moment).

Yogi Bhajan
spiritual behemoth
Sikh power meister
part Muslim, part Hindu
part Buddhist, part bad boy
teaching a discipline
of strength and endurance.

One winter solstice
camped at a trailer park
halfway between
DisneyWorld
and the Kennedy Space Center

*he preached from a street corner
near a black Baptist church.*

*Sunday morning
as the sun rose
on the central Florida plain
the Yogi spewed
ancient Indian tongues
while across the way
the gospel wailed
from deepest Africa.*

Hard to beat that one.

*From sea to sea
the beat went on
an occultural revolution
a youthful counterculture
seeking space
physical and mental
spiritual and political
and of the heart.*

*Robert Monroe's
JOURNEYS OUT OF THE BODY
David Carradine's
KUNG FU
Paramahansa Yogananda's
AUTOBIOGRAPHY OF A YOGI
Phillip Kapleau's
THREE PILLARS OF ZEN.*

*This last
most intriguing
with clinical descriptions
first person accounts
of the White Light
striking the unsuspecting
meditators and moderators*

*students of zen
and collectors of garbage
some in temple
with their roshi
others on subways
reading the newspaper.*

*A blazing beacon
a complete
(but temporary)
liberation
infusing the body
the mind
with the weightlessness
carelessness
consciouslessness
needed
to transcend
to leap
past the mundane
into the realm
of total release
and completion.*

*The descriptions were
fascinating
compelling
riveting
evidence of
the FACT
that this could
DID!
happen
to ordinary people
something so clearly
tangible
beyond
out of reach
but not to be reached for.*

*It became a goal
to strive for
a phenomenon
to study
an experience
to crave*

*But the masters warned
precisely that craving
that reaching
that striving
was the surest barrier
to getting...
... where?*

The Deep Dark

And then there's the Dark.

Sitting in
that impossibly warm
JCC pool
a year comes back
1979
Three Mile Island
a light of its own
the opposite of white
of huge concerts
at Madison Square Garden
then mass demonstrations
and the loss of a lover
I thought was a soul mate.

Amidst the confusion
and the stress
too little sleep
too much madness
demon depression
came down hard
for the first time
a glimpse
a plunge
most unwelcome.

The Deep Dark.

Too many times
through that year
I could not see
how I'd make it
through the night.

Pain
confusion
futility
hopelessness
a void so strong
an abyss so total
endless
infinite
swallowing
black hole
made life itself
the ultimate burden.

A good night's sleep?
A good day's work?
How?
Where?
When?

"Tecumseh's Curse"

*A spiritual friend
John of the stars
astrologer extraordinaire
became my guide
mapped a way out.*

*On December 31, 1980
my 35th birthday
the two big planets
Saturn and Jupiter
would cross paths
in the sky
as they do
every twenty years.*

*A powerful conjunction
for the ages.*

*In ancient days
this mystic meeting
meant a time
of karmic cleansing.*

*A stellar collision
of cold, judgmental Saturn
with mighty Jupiter
Lord of Spirit.*

*The Mayans
(said John)
Egyptians
mighty Nigers
ancient Chinese
Native Americans
all the ab-originals
revered
this heavenly sign*

*as a time of
shock
accounting
catharsis
growth.*

*In America
since 1840
every president
elected the year
of this conjunction
died in office.*

*William Henry Harrison
foe of Tecumseh
caught pneumonia
at his inauguration
died
one month later.*

*So they called it
"Tecumseh's Curse".*

*Abe Lincoln, James Garfield
William McKinley
all shot.*

*Warren G. Harding, poisoned.
FDR, down from old age*

*John Kennedy
we all know about that
(or do we?).*

*Ronald Reagan,
shot but not dead
(or was he?).
That we did
not yet know.*

Or the year
2000
and George W. Bush
how to describe
what would happen next?

What we did know:
on December 31
1980
I would meditate
on Martha's Vineyard Island
in the house
of my friends
Peter and Ronni.

And then
at midnight
I'd go out
and sit atop
sweet South Mountain
a Van Gogh hill
facing the ocean
with a 180 view
of the waters of life.

It would be cold
but
it would be clear.

Give Peace a Chance

In early December
in my darkness
I went down
to the island
and to Caroline.

Lucky me!

Sweet, magical blonde
elfin herbalist
past life goddess
put me in touch
with a gentler side
a deeper joy.

Scottish leprechaun
simple
gentle
infinitely kind
we settled in
to a wonderful house
nestled in a blanket
of unexpected snow
a white whale
of a storm
blasting the Vineyard
pristine pure.

Amidst this luxury
this idyll paradise
we hunkered down
to cut through
all the pain
confusion
and discord
of the decades prior
and lifetimes beyond.

*A blanket of white
over a core of dark
hoping to help us
Give peace a chance.*

*Just as we
mutually embraced
in the peace and seclusion
warmth and excitement
of our quest
the horrible happened.*

John Lennon was murdered.

*As the Dolphins
beat the Patriots
on Monday Night Football
Howard Cosell
to his everlasting credit
broke the news
injected some reality
to the games we play
the madness
the twisted
grotesque
pitiful
anguished
senseless
loss
of our brilliant
beloved
Shaman
Beatle.*

Who can fathom it?

Where is the White Light?

Where is ANY light

*when such a sickness
can seize our nation
psychotic assassins
running around
guns in hand
killing at will.*

*To lose a man
a soul
a spirit
a friend
like John Lennon
and let it go
without a total
transformation
only testifies
to how far we have
left to evolve.*

Seeee how they run!

*Mournful now
we readjust
wounded
bleeding
surrounded by snow
and the warmth of our bodies
(whose body now
will keep Yoko warm?)
to find out
what we can.*

*Hour after hour
day after day
we do our meditations.*

*I sit
an hour at a time
four, six, eight hours a day
timed by
a small alarm
my eyes closed
my back to the wall
next to the bed
where we make love.*

*I make a stab
at getting in
to the unknown
getting clear
of what plagues me.*

*The doubt
the gloom
haunting
devastating
pitiless
Dark.*

*Astrologer John
has suggested
and maybe I've read
the best thing to do
might be to
just
sit
there
clear the mind
work toward clarity
toward silence
toward peace
toward balance
and then
at some point
not work at all.*

*What I learn first
what comes to me
is to sit back
and watch...
watch the dialog
watch the monologue
the issues
distractions
people
places
of my life
my realities
memory banks
illusions
passions
diversions
excursions
they all float by
with all their noise
their business
their meaning
their nonsense.*

*The disharmonies
need to be smoothed
then find the space
to sooth themselves.*

I make mental lists.

*The hours
cruise by
my life
my loves
my work
my my.*

Seeeeee how they run.

*Hour after hour
eon after eon
the petty details
and monumental barriers
each in their time
their power
their import
their void
their absurdity
one by one
they pass by
and crumble.*

*Oh, yeah, HIM!
oh, wow, THAT!
oh, amazing, HER!*

*Some I can deal with
they disappear.*

*Others I can't
and file away.*

*Still others
I can only observe
and squirm with embarrassment
or with pleasure
or with nothing at all.*

*As the eons roll by
they all grow
more distant.*

*The days of peace
the hours of sitting
the minutes of magic
the Moments of love
swirl around.*

*It's like cleaning a room
sweeping out a barn
or sitting quietly
many years later
in a hot pool
with the ghost of my father
and the soul of my Mom.*

*Gradually things
fall into order.*

*A misunderstanding there
with a guy on the island
well
we'll work that out
sometime soon
no big deal.*

*Some stuff with my sister
a call to make
a passage to add
to KILLING OUR OWN
the book that will*

*eventually take me
from the island
and from Caroline.*

*But that's for later
in the "hold" file.*

Now is now.

*Gradually
gratefully
one by one
bit by bit
the debris clears
the dust settles
my mind simplifies
in the passionate warmth
of a snowbound island
and the exquisite embrace
of a powerful
gentle
mystical
woman
in a safe
warm
quiet place.*

We should all be so lucky.

Wait for the Sun

But there's a deadline.

December 31
that last evening
end of the day
month
year
eon
as Saturn and Jupiter
embrace
it will be time
for me to leave
this gorgeous cocoon
put on
four pairs of pants
two pairs of sox
some sweaters
a couple of hats
and wander out
a crazed pilgrim
to the very top
of that freezing hill
pure South Mountain
to look for the stars
as they kiss
then wait
for the sun
to rise over the ocean
and a mind
hopefully facing
where it needs to go.

Christ/Buddha! Christ/Buddha!

*In the last few days
as the mundane realities
of a complex life
settle away
a path clears.*

*It leads to
a single
essential
unresolvable
contradiction:*

*How is it
that the Masters teach
that the Universe is perfect
as it should be
must be
ever was
ever will be
as when Buddha
saw the White Light.*

*But
at the same time
our world is
an unjust
bloody
bigoted
violent
mess
demanding activism
protests
organizing
and fierce Jesus
sweeping the money changers
out of the Temple
resisting the Romans*

*preaching that Sermon
on the Mount.*

*An activist testament
for the Ages.*

*But why
if the universe is perfect
as Buddha found
sitting peacefully
is there a need
for Christ
to make that speech
and mount the cross?*

*In my feeble
undeveloped
naive mind
it all boiled down
to cartoon figures:
Christ the activist
Buddha the meditator.*

*Buddha finding
peace profound
his perfect mind
in a clear
drop of water
settled on a leaf
veiny and green
while the equally evolved
activist Christ
crossed them all
the powers that be
the Romans
the Sanhedran
profane stockbrokers
yuppie cynics
and lost his life
in a sea of pain.*

*Seeing it all
come full circle
as Buddhist monks
burned themselves
Christ-like
in the streets of Saigon
to protest
the invasion
of a Christian army
one must ask:*

Where the intersection?

*If the world is perfect
why fight?*

*If not
how to justify
sitting silent
in mere meditation
letting the world
go to hell
while making a point
of doing nothing?*

*Somewhere deep
in the late night tide
of December 31
1980
in the fortieth hour
of sitting cross-legged
on sports-battered knees
it all boiled down
to that one
over-simplified
illogical
unsolvable puzzle:
How can
Jesus the activist*

*and Sidhartha the seeker
both have it right?*

*These warring images
of how the world works
became my zen cohen.*

What to make of them?

*The endless hours
spilled over
to New Year's day.*

*Little stuff
bubbled up
and floated away
from the messy files
and untidy alcoves
of my soul.*

*Distractions here
pleasures there
they came
they went
the conflict
raged.*

*Christ/Buddha
Christ/Buddha
warrior/mystic
warrior/mystic
fight/meditate
fight/meditate
conflict/peace
flawed/perfect
duty/freedom
work/play
being/nothingness
meaning/meaningless.*

*I got
cleaner
clearer
lighter
nowhere.*

*The two balloons
the two men
the two images
the two icons
still at loggerheads.*

*My time to go
to the mountain
came and went.*

Perfect

Then
the distractions
ceased.

What was left
unexamined
that I hadn't turned over
so many times
was too damn boring
to visit again.

But still
no sign.

Another hour
to sit and think
another hour
the mountain can wait.

Then
at last
post-midnight
first overtime
score tied
sudden death
clock running
Buddha and Jesus
eye to eye.

Finally

SUDDENLY

it
(or She)
came…

POOF!

*These two balloons
these two characters
these two worldviews
their conflicted
ideas
ethos
angst
egos
hopelessly separated
bound in illogic*

SUDDENLY

*there came a third
not bigger
not stronger
just the
all-encompassing
all-embracing
 power of*

LOVE

*It came in the form
of a friend.*

*Earlier that year
she had met me
at LAX
as I flew home
from Hawaii.*

*Our swimmer with dolphins
with flaming red hair
lovers we'd been
but now
my sister.*

*We spent some days
doing LA
being siblings
non-bodily lovers
astral dancing.*

*Now
on the Vineyard
here she came
waltzing in
to my mind
right on time
her own balloon
rising up
pouring over
wrapping in light
those of the boys
Christ and Buddha
instantly at peace.*

YES!

*The conflict
ended
(in a draw)
everyone was happy
my red-head friend
really loved me
and that was all
that really
mattered.*

YES!

The contradiction is real.

NO!!

The world can't be both

*perfect
and flawed.
We can't be
simultaneously
active and passive
fighter and at peace.*

*But She came to say
lover and twin
there is a level
where*

NONE OF THAT MATTERS

*and the conflict
between
an imperfect world
and a perfect universe
real
painful
tangible
though it may be
is merely a subset*

OF ANOTHER REALM

*on another plane
which willingly
lovingly
with infinite capacity
and warmth
embraces the dissonance
encircles it
fulfills it
and renders it
harmonious.*

*PERFECT
IN ITS IMPERFECTION*

*within the glorious
all-embracing
circle of love
that needs
no change
while embracing change
endlessly.*

*All this came
in the instant
her face
bubbled up
between the bubbles
and in that instant*

AAAHHH!

it was OVER

*my life to that date
summarized
epitomized
and encoded
in a quick yelp
a shout of relief
as my aching knees
instantly uncrossed
and allowed my body
to fall over left
in sweet release.*

*I had no idea
exactly
what it was.*

*But I did know
what I'd been seeking
for so long
had come at last
and this
particular search
would yield
no more.*

DONE!

DONE DONE DONE!!!

*It was time
at last
to go to the mountain.*

*I was satisfied
happy
lightened
content
in the Moment
ready now
to gaze at the stars
and at the ocean
embrace
the peace
profound
the love
supreme
and simultaneously
in the night's
perfect splendor
freeze my ass off.*

Imagine

*Sitting warm
in that pool
eons later
I looked back
on that time
with deepest gratitude.*

*Caroline moved
off to Ireland
she has two boys
and writes a letter
once a year.*

*I think of her
once a day.*

*My red-haired
cosmic sister
is still a light
unto my soul
we talk regularly
by phone
and e-mail
and love each other
without bound.*

*She never knew
the full impact
of her "visit"
until I sent
an early draft
of this poem.*

*Right after she came
in her balloon
I did go
to South Mountain.*

*Dressed I was
like a thrift shop
four sweaters
four pairs of pants
long underwear
all that froze
were my feet.*

*Two pairs of sox
one of boots
were not enough.*

*In that perfect
New England night
cold and clear
the stars burned white
Saturn and Jupiter
did their dance
exactly where
cosmic John
said to look.*

*In the deepest darkness
before dawn
I saw Lennon
heard him
felt his presence
and his need
the murdered Beatle
so recently ripped
from his body
and I wondered:*

What separates us?

*If physical death
is merely
a door*

*to another reality
then what of us
goes on
and what
goes under?*

*What's lost?
What preserved?*

*I heard him out there
howling
seeking
angry
torn.*

*I felt our pain
and our rage...*

and our Love.

*And then
came dawn
red
clear
gorgeous
and then...*

*orange
warmer.*

That Magic Bus

*Liftetimes later
one day after
we buried Mom
I shuffled to
my parents' house
of 35 years
the earthly focus
of their lives
and in their bedroom
I lay down
wanting to cry
wanting to feel
all the sadness
all the loss
I'd felt with Lennon
on that hilltop
years before.*

*Amidst their pictures
their pillows
the toothbrushes
the neckties
the minutiae of
their daily lives
now cut short
I lay face down
on their bed
hour after hour
asking for answers.*

*At the dimming
of the day
I felt them both
warm glowing orbs
in the room
seeing nothing
but feeling*

*their presence
on my back
a warmth
a love
tangible
clear
it HAD to be them.*

*But was it
REALLY?*

*Who were they
NOW?*

*Was Dad's spirit
still missing
the five teeth
he lost
playing racquetball?*

*Could Mom
now walk
since the body she wore
crippled by cancer
was six feet under?*

*If the death of the ego
opens the door
to Enlightenment
the White Light that awaits
absolute detachment
the supremely elegant
moment of liberation
from the earthly
and mundane...*

*then how is that different
from physical death
that white light tunnel*

*so many describe
who come back?*

*If it was really
Mom and Dad
warming my back
that August evening
did they also
when they were done
make me feel
in no uncertain terms
that I was not
to spend the night?*

*Or was it just
that part
of me
that wanted to sleep
at home
in my bed
conjuring the image
of disembodied voices
to tell me what
I wanted to hear?*

*Those who believe
in hellfire and damnation
may well get
exactly that
when they go.*

*Those who believe
in reincarnation
in one evolving life
after the other
followed by
eternal peace
once all karma
is worked out…*

is that for us?

*Can those who die
really and truly
howl away
to a freezing seeker
on a Vineyard night
or rub the back
of a grieving son?*

*If reincarnation is real
exactly who rides
that magic bus
to a new body
when that first one
is dead and gone?*

Who drives?

Who pays?

Who takes the tokens?

*Or are we all
just tiny fish
swimming the rapids
up the stream
of karmic evolution?*

*The collective
consciousness
of our species:*

*could it be
a mere toy
given carelessly
to a child
of some grand
super-conscious race?*

*Our blue-green planet
our fleshly beings
and evolving souls
are they just
a clever device
to create
a tiny flash
to briefly amuse
some supra child?*

*The light
can come
however we
in our yeasting
choose to make it:*

*with a nuclear holocaust
a tiny flash
in the cosmic
scheme of things…*

*or an ecological catastrophe
a global fry
but a tiny flash
in the cosmic
scheme of things…*

*or a collective enlightenment
a species-wide
ecstatic embrace
of conscious liberation
a tiny flash
nonetheless
as we all sing
(along with John)
"love, love, love …
love is all you need."*

I like that last one!

*That shout of joy
those uncrossing knees
the days of embrace
that freezing night
all cleared a path
for that flash
of inexpressible White.*

*"Here it is"
my parents said
"here's what's in store
when you pass
don't be afraid
don't mourn for us
it's alright
we're okay
we'll see you soon
don't worry
be happy."*

*Those dark nights
of the soul
tropical depressions
the smell of hell
shocks to the soul
the nagging sense
that something's missing.*

*They all stay
but now
they all fit.*

*"Trade all you have
or might have been
for one small breath
of ecstasy."*

*DEAL!
DONE!*

What Drops Away

*Amidst the ecstasy
and release
comes the realization
of a brighter circle.*

*There is indeed
a Big Light.*

*It forever burns
in its good time
spinning round
at apparent odds
with the darkest nights
of the soul.*

*But two are one
dark and light
they cannot exist
without each other.*

*What matters more
is that they
 are contradictory subsets
of a larger reality
logical impossibilities
taken separately
but a fused whole
when known as one.*

*This yin/yang test
is not about
light or dark
but the line around
the space beyond.*

*Our world has embraced
both Christ and Buddha*

*activist and passivist.
They are separate
but inseparable.*

*The deep dark
of demon depression
clearly exists
but must yield
in its time
to the Big Light
and then
vice-versa.*

*The spinning takes us
further on
further out
further toward
whatever it is
wherever it is
we have to go
and getting there
may require
just forgetting
what we think we know
and thought we saw.*

*What drops away
is not the sense
of light or dark
but the discomfort
of constantly questioning
one's own place
in the universe.*

*It's night
or it's day
but here we are.*

Whatever comes next...

*The afternoon wore on
the Big Light
did not fade
it was digested
and ate me too.*

*I swam the rest
of my laps
the second
108.*

*It was either
the Jewish one
or Buddhist one
Muslim one
or Christian one
the pagan one
or Hindu one
I don't remember
I didn't know then.*

*All I could feel
of my body
in the heat
and the wet
was my calf
cramping away
making sure
I didn't disappear
altogether.*

*And in that transition
back to the body
amidst the questioning
the wonderings
about*

*ego
soul
spirit
mind
it came down
like the dawn...*

*My parents
my family
those dearest friends
who saw me through
are angels
white lights
spinning
in a wheel
where dark must return
then disappear again
in the bright.*

*The hug of an infant
on a beach
the loss of a parent
the taste of a soul mate
the smell of spring...*

*the eternal need
for absolute love
from other humans
means to me
there can be
no liberation
or release
except through the joy
and the agony
of human indivisibility
discovered alone
and in concert.*

*Perfectly loved
perfectly loving
loving self
loving others
can it be otherwise?*

What else is there?

*A liberation
a burden
welcome them both.*

*The brights are blinding
as are the darks
the lens is clear
the realities stark
the contrast beautiful.*

*It would seem
simply
(but what do I know?
I'm just an amateur!)
that we are all
in this together.*

Bound we are.

*No one
gets out of here
alive
alone
alight
a light
except
ALL of us.*

*We are
immutably
a collective consciousness.*

*There is separation
between us each
and our planet.*

*But the stronger reality
is the quantum physic
that embraces
and transcends
all the dissonance
and divisions.*

*It is the continuity
the essential
one-ness
the indivisibility
that we seek
and flee
and then embrace.*

*It swallows
and digests
the dark/white contradictions
that spin the wheel.*

*The flashes of ecstasy
the depths of dark
and what transcends them
makes them each
fleeting preview
enticing confirmation
for when we evolve
as a species
and all are fed
warm
respected
connected....*

*Then ALL of us
and ONLY all of us
might just fly
at childhood's end
with our bodies
and our globe
with our genius
and our bliss
separately and together
from our own
cold, clear mountain
or our warm
Big Light pool
into the realm…*

of whatever comes next…

Thanks for reading this…
Light & Love…
Harvey Wasserman

Also by Harvey Wasserman:

HARVEY WASSERMAN'S HISTORY OF THE UNITED STATES
Introduced by Howard Zinn
(www.harveywasserman.com)

THE LAST ENERGY WAR:
THE BATTLE OVER UTILITY DEREGULATION
(www.sevenstories.com)

ENERGY WAR:
REPORTS FROM THE FRONT

AMERICA BORN & REBORN:
THE CYCLES OF US HISTORY

Coming soon:
THE SPIRAL OF US HISTORY
(www.harveywasserman.com)

Coming soon:
SOLARTOPIA:
THE FUTURE OF ENERGY
(www.harveywasserman.com)

Columns and Reportage appearing at www.freepress.org.

With Bob Fitrakis:

ANOTHER STOLEN ELECTION:
VOICES OF THE DISENFRANCHISED, 2004
(www.freepress.org)

IMPRISON GEORGE W. BUSH:
COMMENTARY ON WHY THE PRESIDENT MUST BE INDICTED
(www.freepress.org)

GEORGE W. BUSH VS. THE SUPERPOWER OF PEACE
(www.freepress.org)

With Dan Juhl:

HARVESTING WIND ENERGY AS A CASH CROP:
A GUIDE TO LOCALLY-OWNED WIND POWER
(www.danmar.us)

With Norman Solomon, Bob Alvarez & Eleanor Walters:

KILLING OUR OWN:
THE DISASTER OF AMERICA'S EXPERIENCE WITH ATOMIC RADIATION
Introduction by Dr. Benjamin Spock

With Dan Keller (documentary films):

LOVE JOY'S NUCLEAR WAR
THE LAST RESORT (www.gmpfilms.com)

From Lee Waters:

LEAKED SECRET TRANSCRIPTS FROM BUSH'S OVAL OFFICE, 2002-2004
(www.freepress.org)

Coming soon: From Thomas Paine:

THE SECRET LIFE OF DANIEL SHAYS
(www.harveywasserman.com)

www.ingramcontent.com/pod-product-compliance
Lightning Source LLC
Chambersburg PA
CBHW022132080426
42734CB00006B/334